A Test of Faith

When Life Doesn't go to Plan

by
Fr Benedict J. Groeschel, CFR.

*All booklets are published thanks to the
generous support of the members of the
Catholic Truth Society*

CATHOLIC TRUTH SOCIETY
PUBLISHERS TO THE HOLY SEE

Contents

All rights reserved. This abridged edition © Copyright 2017 The Incorporated Catholic Truth Society, 40-46 Harleyford Road London SE11 5AY Tel: 020 7640 0042 Fax: 020 7640 0046.

Originally published as 'Arise from Darkness' © Copyright 1995 Ignatius Press, San Francisco.

ISBN 978 1 78469 163 9

Chapter 1

Arise From Darkness

A guide - not an answer

This book is not an answer but a guide to those in darkness. It is about going on in spite of darkness, about survival, and about using the unavoidable dark times of life to grow. There is actually nothing new in what I suggest. The solution, not the answer, that I will try to enunciate is found in the gospel and in the lives of great saints, heroes and heroines, and in the lives of very brave ordinary people whom we all have known. Many guides have been written for people struggling with the mystery of evil. It is the theme of much of the great literature of the human race. But in each generation the question returns; each age has its own dark background in front of which the struggle to keep going and find meaning must be worked out. In every age, men, women, and children not only ask "Why?" but ask "How am I going to go on to arise from darkness?" It is that which my book will address.

Who should or should not read this book?

Some readers may be saying to themselves: "This is too heavy for me right now. Things are going fairly well, and I hope they will continue to go well." If you feel that way, don't read this book now. Put it aside for a day when you may need it. Others will say: "Things are going well for me now, but I would like to be compassionate to others, to share their grief even though my life is fairly tranquil." You may wish to share this book with someone now in the incredible darkness that eventually comes upon us all.

However, this book is written expressly for those going through a time of darkness and pain. I have tried to look at the question "Why?", and I have found only partial answers. I am convinced that believers who are unafraid to pay the price will know what to do though they are unable to understand why this is all happening. The what is much more likely to be found than the why is to be answered.

The what cannot be said in a sentence or a few paragraphs. It is experienced in the single intuition of the Cross, the vision of Calvary and the resurrection, but this vision must be drawn out into words and applied to the difficult situations that are likely to cause darkness and pain. Picture yourself at night in a dark wood; far ahead of you is a light. Everything else is darkness. There is no doubt about what way to go - toward the light. But between you and the light there is unknown terrain - ditches, brambles, perhaps a barbed wire fence. How do you find the way to the light? You are exhausted, frightened, inclined just to sit there in the dark in hopes that the sky will lighten. You can just wait.

But if you are moved to challenge the darkness, to arise, to follow the light, to find the way, to move on with the precious time of life, then this book is written for you.

The first step - getting over the big lie

There is an incredible untruth communicated to children as they grow up in our technologically advanced world, namely, that most people have a good chance of living out their lives without times of suffering or pain, times of darkness. This illusion is created by the media, especially by advertising (a world of happy endings), by education, by generalised attitudes that make up the social customs of our people, and even by our religious thinking. Everyone's life is supposed to be filled with sunshine; and when it is not, luck will change, things will work out well, and the sunny carefree times will return. Not to worry - all will be roses.

This untruth is not a deliberate lie - in fact it is the universal denial of reality. It is not a deception to be condemned but an illusion to be dispelled. We must do this if we are ever to arrive at any mature sense of relative peace and security in this world. Every person reading these lines will have had some real experiences of darkness in life already, and all will have more unless they die soon. Many are in darkness now, and that's why they have picked up this book. If one does not face this very obvious fact - that times of suffering, pain, and difficulty are inevitable - one will run neurotically through life like a frightened animal. One is likely to become disillusioned and deeply depressed or cynical or filled with a brooding anger. Very likely this anger will be aimed at God; he should have made the world a better place.

If we do not run away from trouble or attempt to avoid it completely, then what are we to do? Obviously the first thing is to have a conviction, a mindset, that trouble and pain are inevitable parts of life. They come to all, especially to those who try desperately to protect themselves from suffering. The most bitterly disappointed people are those who thought that this brief, fragile life was going to bring them the joy reserved for the blessed in heaven.

Once you have rejected the illusion that life is really delightful for most people (and you hoped to be included among them), then you are prepared to face dark times. Some decide to do this by a stoic determination, generally maintaining a dignified silence and trying to avoid involving others in their pain. This attitude may lead to a certain maturity, but it can also lead to a quiet hopelessness, a humourless and bleak approach to life. A stoical friend of mine described life as a journey from obscurity to oblivion. This appraisal omits an appreciation of our own eternal vocation, which brings us beyond the sorrows of this world.

The obvious fact is that everyone suffers and that almost all go through periods of deep suffering and darkness. Some, inexplicably, seem to experience more suffering than others. If you are in darkness, recognise the fact that you have plenty of company. If you have failed to admit the universal human experience of suffering, then this recognition should make you more compassionate and sensitive to people's hidden pain in the future. By rejecting the unwarranted illusion that "everyone is doing well but me", you will become a far more open human being, sensitive to the sufferings of others, and willing to listen and help. What is far more important, you will not look on this Christian way of acting as a chore or burden. Even if things are going well, compassionate concern for others will constantly remind you that life is not always sunshine. In a wounded world marked by the mystery of the original fall of the human race, life cannot always be beautiful, but it can be filled with meaning.

To arise means to go beyond

It is not enough merely to survive the trials of life; it is necessary to go beyond them. In the moment of unforeseen grief any thought of growing through pain is usually incomprehensible. The suggestion alone may cause anger and be resisted. But the intense anger, which is a predictable response to threat, will give way to a decision to go on, to live with the sorrow and even to grow from it. This is what the saints mean by the mystery of the Cross, a mystery essentially linked to the resurrection. Just as Easter is meaningless without Calvary, Calvary is incomprehensible without the victory of the empty tomb.

If you are reading this book in the intense moment of grief, you need to discipline yourself just to hold on, to survive mutely and without understanding why. But if your suffering has subsided a bit and you have lived with it for a time and are trying to take up your responsibilities to others, to put the pieces back together, you need to ponder the mystery of the Cross.

The message of the death and resurrection of Christ is this: with faith we can go repeatedly on in this life by using defeat and loss as an opportunity to challenge God's grace to help us survive. In Genesis 32, Jacob wrestled with the angel of God in the darkness. Although wounded and limping, he received the blessing and went on his way. St Paul's boast amid his sufferings and disappointments expresses so well the mystery of the Cross (*2 Co* 11:21-12:10) All we have to be proud of, to claim as our own, is our weakness and failures, but we can boast "in the Cross of our Lord Jesus Christ" (*Ga* 6:14). When we are knocked down and defeated by life, abandoned by friends, betrayed by those we thought we could rely on, weary of our own foolishness or even facing death, that is when we can pick up the Cross and wave it at grief, sadness, and death. To boast in the Cross, it seems to me, is an almost fierce gesture when we confront all that would defeat us and say: "Look at the Cross, all of you, and know that I shall not be overcome, because the Lord of Life is with me and in me, and he will go with me even through the valley of the shadow of death."

Chapter 2

When Friends Fail

In the Gospel of John we read these most sorrowful words of the Saviour at the Last Supper: "The hour is coming, indeed it has come, when you will be scattered, every man to his home, and will leave me alone" (16:32). Jesus is speaking to his disciples and predicting that, despite their protestation of loyalty to him, they are all about to leave him alone. Why did Jesus Christ experience the absence, the betrayal, the failure of his friends? How could they have failed him? Why did they do this to one who had been so good to them? Many Christian writers have seen that in his Passion, Christ endures every suffering, every pain, every humiliation, every sorrow that can come to human beings. As a result Christ must suffer even this - to be betrayed by his friends, to be left alone. This he must endure so that we will know that God has taken upon himself all human pain and suffering.

The experience of having friends fail comes to us all. This most painful experience of life can include the loss of family, parents, spouses, and children, as well as dear friends. Suddenly we are left alone. I am not implying that these loved ones fail us on purpose or that they are necessarily at fault. Many times friends fail to be there for us simply because they are human. Perhaps they have died. We desperately need them, and they are not there because death has taken them away. There isn't an adult who doesn't know what I am writing about. We long for the support on which we relied from loved ones, and they're gone. If we have a strong, sturdy faith we can say, "Oh, yes, they are praying for me on the other side", and we're right. But you can't sit down and have a cup of coffee with them. You can't call them on the phone and say, "What a day!"

We change

People fail us for other reasons. First of all, friends change and we change. Did you ever sit down and count all the friends that you've lost simply because they changed or you changed? In all circumstances of life, friends change. It's no one's fault. My best friend in high school also became a priest, but he's changed; he's no longer a priest. We meet every few years, catch up on things, but our lives are incredibly different - our goals and purposes are far apart.

The loss of friends is most painful in family relationships. Children grow up together. They enjoy everything together; they suffer, weep, laugh, and play together, and the years go on. In this age brothers and sisters may live on different continents, worlds apart. They meet years later, and they hardly know each other. In a certain sense, we can say that there once was a friendship and now it's gone, leaving just a biological relationship. If you add to competitiveness the disputes over property and inheritances or simple jealousy, then you can understand how what was once a family becomes simply a festering wound. What was once a bond of love becomes a chain of hate.

We lose loved ones also because of resentment. We all want to be loved in a special way, and sometimes our relatives, even our closest relatives, or our best friends don't love us in the special way that we think we need. And why do we need that? Because we're self-centred. We have no right to be so special in the way that we demand, but when we don't get this desired special attention we turn away.

The recognition of friends

Sometimes we recognise real friends only when they are departing or are already gone. How really hidden we all are from each other. "How are you?" "Oh, fine." We could be dying and we would say, "Oh, fine."

When you are with the poor and you ask someone, "How are you?" and he's dying, he says, "I'm dying. I'm scared." In the suburbs when you ask, "How are you?" he says, "Oh, I'm fine. I have cancer of the brain, but I'm fine." We are usually afraid to tell even our friends the truth about ourselves because we are afraid to lose them. We're afraid to share the very things that would bring others closer to us and us closer to them. We are afraid to share our sufferings. We might recall that our Lord Jesus Christ was not afraid to share his sufferings. He still shares them. That's what a crucifix is about.

The loss of the Son of God

Separation from loved ones and friends is, then, something that happened to the Son of God. Think of the Son of God, the second Person of the Trinity, as a Divine Person, not yet son of Mary, but simply Son of God.

Along with his separation from his Father, Jesus experienced the failings and shortcomings of his human friends. His boyhood acquaintances and friends in Nazareth attempted to kill him. These were his neighbours in a small, isolated country town. Many of them were related to him. They took him to the brow of the hill to throw him off.

The failure of the apostles at the end of his life is incredible. It is almost beyond imagination. How in the world did those men who lived with him for three years completely desert him in his hour of need? Oh, yes, John came back after fleeing, but we forget that there were some hours when they were all gone. He was left completely alone when he was tried, scourged, crowned with thorns, and condemned to death…all alone.

Our Lord was abandoned by his disciples while his faithful followers, almost all women, could offer practically no comfort because of the social customs. He was there all alone. His lonely death follows upon the pathetic scene in the Garden where he is abandoned by his apostles, who fall asleep when he needs them desperately.

Part of the human condition

Has this happened to you? This is an even more painful question - have you ever fallen asleep on a friend who needed you? That's the haunting question for us all. I know when people have failed me, but I usually can't recognise when I have failed them. Why did Christ go through all this? He did it for you and me so that we will have an example to guide us when we are left alone, one of the most common and painful situations of life. We can know that Jesus Christ has been there before us. His example will give us the wisdom to ask objectively, "Why do friends fail?" Because we are human. Because we have original sin. Because we grow old and weak and are sick and are preoccupied with keeping ourselves together. Why did the apostles fail? Because this was all too much for them. It was beyond their strength. Be prepared for friends to fail you and also for the special grief when someone will say to you, "You failed me."

There are wonderful souls in the world who never failed anyone, and God has blessed them. But even they will die and not be there. It is part of the human condition that we all experience the failure of friends, of loved ones, of spouses, of parents, of children. Some of those who read these lines have suffered the failure of their parents. I think it is the most painful suffering one can go through in this life.

Better to love and lose

Be warned - love and you will get hurt. But it is better for us to love and lose than not to love at all because we are all moving toward an everlasting experience of love. When life does not make sense, the believer must recall that we are moving toward a much more real and everlasting experience of love.

Two critical realisations

We don't like to think about the inescapable fact that human life is a quickly passing experience, a river swiftly moving. Part of the answer to the question "What do we do when life doesn't make sense?" is the recognition of that fact. We need to grasp that all things we experience, even the most precious, the love of family and friends, are passing. Any harm or pain that the failure of loved ones brings us is also passing. Life does not simply pass. It goes on into something more beautiful or more terrible, to salvation or to eternal loss. Life's purpose and our attitude toward it must be defined by this conviction if we are believers. We will return to this crucial fact over and over.

The second realisation is that Christ has endured and sanctified the pain of the failure of friends by his own life and by his forgiveness of them for their failures. He reproached them, but he did not abandon them. He responded to Peter's protestation of unending loyalty at the Last Supper by saying, "Simon, Simon, behold Satan has demanded to have you, that he might sift you like wheat, but I have prayed for you that your faith may not fail; and when you have turned again, strengthen your brothers...I tell you, Peter, the cock will not crow this day, until you three times deny that you know me" (*Lk* 22:31-34).

How does one, in practice, put these two ideas together - the passing nature of human experience and the forgiving example of Christ? By the mystics, the answer is called the mystery of the Cross. This mystery is not an abstract intellectual idea or argument but an experienced reality. One can enter into the fullness of this mystery only when one is in fact suffering or has suffered. In this case we are looking at the failure of friends. We see that Christ endures this failure and overcomes this pain in two ways - he forgives Peter ahead of time on the eve of the Passion before the events take place. He then embraces the sorrow but also shows that his Father will bring good out of evil.

The Changeless Friend

We have all experienced the failure of friends. For one reason or another they were not there when we needed them. We know that no matter what happens, if we turn to him, there is one Friend who never fails, who is always there. Our faith constantly brings us to that Changeless Friend. Prayer is essential here because it is the only way for us to encounter our Friend. He is changeless because he no longer walks in this world of change. Through him we come into contact with that multitude of friends who have gone before us to that bright world where he waits for us - his Father's house. Even if you have to pray in pain or agony as he did in the Garden, you will soon enough find him there in the shadows. Prayer, deep personal prayer coming from the heart of our being, is the way that we can embrace and be embraced by our Changeless Friend.

Chapter 3

When Our Security Is Threatened

What do we do when life doesn't make sense because our economic or personal security is threatened or even taken away? We are well aware that in this life our Lord Jesus Christ had little or no security. Certainly from the beginning he had no personal security as we understand it. "After the Wise Men had left, the angel of the Lord appeared in a dream to Joseph and said, 'Get up, and take the child and his mother and go as fast as you can into Egypt, and stay there. For Herod will soon be looking for the child to kill him'" (*Mt* 2:13).

The life of Christ began with danger, and insecurity followed him every step of the way. Economic uncertainty was his constant companion. Furthermore he did nothing to encourage people who had possessions to feel secure in this world. In fact, if anything, he actively discouraged feelings of security. The message of Christ's parables and his life is this: if you are trying to make some sense out of life, it is important to decide that worldly or material security is an illusion. Decide today that if you are seeking security and a perfectly safe situation in this life, you are pursuing something that is in itself very insecure - even unreal.

A false sense of security

Insecurity and uncertainty are facts of life. Obviously, people have a right to some economic security from what they can earn by work and careful spending. However, this right is more properly seen as our obligation to take care of ourselves so as not to be a burden to others. What has happened in the rich nations is that security has become a false god. When I studied psychology twenty-five years ago, personnel directors commented that graduates fresh out of college were looking for jobs and inquiring about the retirement policy. Above all else they had a need to be secure. That feeling of security turned out to be a fraud. It caused people to forget that our worldly accomplishments are certainly passing and temporary. Nothing could be more obvious than the fact that we are not permanently here. If you feel secure in this world, you feel secure unwisely and are clinging to a shadow. Our economic superiority over some other nations causes us to have these false feelings of security.

Even if a person were to have a great deal of apparent economic security, what about health? What about the peculiar vicissitudes of life? What about the hundreds of possible calamities that could come in an instant to cause one to lose one's security? Loss of employment, loss of one's own home, danger to health, aging, and, in the later years of life, chronic illness - these are all things that reveal the lie underlying a false sense of earthly security. What is the answer?

A sense of peace when insecure

The obvious answer is Christ's teaching not to put your trust in possessions. It is not wrong to feel a little more comfortable when we are more secure than we were. That's fine. I suppose the Christ Child may have felt a little more safe and sound when Joseph and Mary got back to their home in Nazareth after Herod was dead. It is by no means wrong to enjoy a bit of security and peace of mind, but don't put your ultimate trust in anything that passes away. Don't be surprised when your earthly security is threatened, because it is really always tenuous, but we simply don't realise it. Since security in this world is called into question every day, by illness, mishap, and accident, what then should we do? We need to follow the example of Christ and trust in God alone. This will permit us to have peace and trust in God even when we experience insecurity, because we already know that any sense of security in this world is an illusion.

What trust in God really means

Trust in God does not mean that everything is going to work out just the way we want it to, that everything is going to be peaches and cream. Trust in God doesn't mean that he is going to restore the false sense of security that we had before. It means that, whatever happens, we believe that God is there with us and that, if we cling to him, he will bring good out of evil, even out of the evil that he has only permitted to happen. I must make up my mind now that in the darkest hour of life, I will believe that God is with me. And I believe that he will be with you and all who turn to him and even with those who do not know enough to turn to him. This life at its best or worst passes quickly, but God is always there. In the end, the good and the bad walk over the very narrow threshold of physical death. They pass beyond the veil of physical appearances and are standing in the presence of God, where each must render an account and rely on God's mercy.

Real security in the real world

We need to believe that on the other side of this very thin material wall, the world we perceive with our senses, there is a world without time or ambiguity. It is a world no longer in the process of dying. In this world we are temporarily in a place of incompleteness, of adventure, of partial illusion. Though incomprehensible, the possibilities of the next world are very clear. There is either an eternal life or an eternal loss. I don't know about you, but I do not wish to perish forever. I suspect that you, like myself, want to see your dear ones in the eternal life of the next world. I am sure that, like everyone else, you do not want the good things that you have cherished in this life to disappear forever. The message of the glorious resurrection of Jesus Christ is that what we have loved will not disappear, that the good things will last forever. That hope is the meaning of trust in God. Many Christians in the course of the centuries, including many members of the clergy and religious orders, have trusted in this world and at the same time have tried to trust in eternity. They've had a foot in both camps. It's a mistake. Cardinal Wolsey, who had served King Henry VIII so faithfully, as he was dying in Henry's disfavour, is supposed to have said, "Had I served my God as well as I have served my king, he would not have left me in my old age, naked to my enemies." Yes, he, like all too many others, tried to have a stake in both worlds.

Some suggestions

First of all, get your priorities in order. I know that most readers are sensibly concerned about their economic security. Others are concerned about their physical health. The important thing is to put your treasure where it ought to be. Repeat to yourselves the words of Christ, "Lay up for yourselves treasures in heaven, where neither moth nor rust consumes and thieves do not break in and steal" (*Mt* 6:20). We owe it to ourselves, and we need to give an example to our families and friends, many of whom have become incredibly materialistic. We need to remind them by frugality in our use of things, by modesty in what we wear, and by the plainness of things we use. If you are a Christian, you need to live as one who, convinced that here we have no lasting city, is seeking the Kingdom of God.

Second, we need to overcome our feelings of financial insecurity by generosity. It is necessary to be generous when you are secure and even when your security is threatened. If you have a little to give, give it joyously. Remember the poor widow whom Christ praised because she gave all that she had into the temple treasury.

Third, we need to give an example of generosity. An old priest who is not well does his Christmas shopping in a few minutes and at the same time gives a great example to all his family. He sends me labels for all his relatives and friends and gives me money to buy meals for poor people in the name of each one of them. All the relatives get a letter saying that Father Ed arranged to pay for a meal for a poor person in their name on Christmas Day. These notes bring with them not only the prayers of the poor and of our community but also a good example.

"Do not lay up for yourselves treasures on earth, where moth and rust consume and thieves break in and steal, but lay up for yourselves treasures in heaven…" (*Mt* 6:19-20). These are words not of St Paul, not of St John, not of St Peter. These are the words of Jesus Christ. They are powerful and awesome words. Those who have followed these words will have a security that no one can take from them. They will know where they are and where they are going while the world does not know where it is or where it is going. We are standing right next to an invisible wall. And on the other side of that wall is an eternal reality. Modern people are worried about their security. Well they may worry, because their world is quickly slipping into paganism, and the blindness it brings is about the true meaning of life.

What we should worry about

We need to be insecure about the right things. I am very insecure about the fact that I have not spoken up enough against evil. I'm insecure at times that I have gone along with evil in a passive sort of way. I know that on Judgment Day I will be asked about these things. But I am not insecure about the things of this world. It is harder for a lay person than for me. I'm a friar. One day I had a hole in my sock, so someone gave me a few dollars to buy a pair of socks. Our little community is trying to take St Francis seriously. We don't save up. We don't have any real estate. And yet we are secure. We are not worried. The Lord will provide. If at any moment we friars decided we'd better start investing money and saving our funds, then I would be frightened; but I am not frightened now, because we have relied on the Lord.

In your life, especially as a lay person, or as a diocesan priest, or as a member of a religious community that runs an institution, you cannot rely on the Lord in the same way. But you personally must rely on him. If you trust in the funds of this world, if you trust in worldly possessions, you will be deceived. You will be ripped off. Even if you have lots of worldly possessions when you die, you will be cheated by all of them. Your own possessions will cheat you. They are the biggest cheat of all. They are

fool's gold. Rich or poor, a good Christian is generous and is most of all reliant on God. St Paul, who had nothing when he travelled around the world, earning his daily bread as a tentmaker, preaching and asking for little, wrote, "I am sure that neither death, nor life, nor angels, nor principalities, nor powers, nor things present, nor things to come, nor height, nor depth, nor anything else in all creation, can separate us from the love of God in Christ Jesus, our Lord" (*Rm* 8: 38-39). And that - and nothing else - is security.

Chapter 4

When The Church Lets Us Down

Scarcely a week goes by that people do not tell me that the Church or some representative of the Church has failed them and even hurt them badly. Sometimes these wounded Christians are sad, but more frequently they are very angry. Occasionally they forget that neither I nor any other priest nor any bishop represents the entire Church. It is painful for them and painful for us. To tell the truth, probably the closer one is to the Church the more one is likely to be hurt by the Church. I suspect that the person in the world who is most often hurt by the Church is the pope himself, for he is constantly under criticism from all sides - not only from the attacks of those outside the Church, but also from the disgruntled complaints of those within it. The question arises for all of us from Pope to parishioner, "How can the Church fail us so often and still be the Mystical Body of Christ?" Surely we are justified in expecting better care of us from the historical representative of the loving Saviour of the world.

Part of our problem is that we use this expression "the Church" to describe a number of things that are related but are to some degree quite different from one another. Obviously the word church means different things. It can simply mean a building. It can mean a particular denomination, like the Congregational Church. It can mean a parish or a diocese. "I got in trouble with the local church." It can mean everybody in the world who is a Christian, or it can mean everyone in the world who is a Catholic, a member of the "Catholic Church". The word catholic means "universal", from the Greek words *kata holos*, that is, "from out of the whole universe".

The body of Christ

First of all, it means the Mystical Body of Christ spoken of so powerfully by St Paul. "For no man ever hates his own flesh but nourishes it and cherishes it, as Christ does the Church, for we are members of his body" (*Ep* 5:29-30). There is a spiritual reality that stands behind the visible Church, the Body of Christ united in a profoundly spiritual way with all of his members.

Most of the time, when we say "the Church", we mean the visible, external Church led by the bishops and the pope and also all the other people who have responsibility, the clergy, religious, the active laity, the parish council, the St Vincent de Paul Society, and so forth. Someone says, "I work for the Church." "Who do you work for?" They say, "St Mary's Hospital". That's "the Church". "I work for the Church and they're cheap." Does it mean the chancery or diocesan office, or is it their parish? These are a whole series of questions that you want to keep in mind when people say that "the Church" failed them. Usually, when people say that the Church failed them, they mean their parish, or the diocese, or even the diocesan bishop. They may also mean for example the Church in the United States.

Whatever the meaning, almost everyone reading this book can say, "The Church has failed me." It could be the parish, the diocese, the Catholic school, an institution within the Church, a Catholic publication, or the bishops. Everyone can make that claim. The possibilities of being hurt are enormous, and they are greater the more one is involved. For example, generous people come to the Church looking for an opportunity to serve, to give substantially of their time and energy. Maybe they give their whole lives in religious vocations. For years things go well, and they are appreciated or at least given the opportunity to work hard and get something done. And then there is a changing of the guard. New leaders come in, and those of the "old guard" are in the way. Little regard is given to all they have done with little or no personal recognition. The feeling comes over them that God himself has no regard for what they have done. They become, understandably but unwisely, angry at God, or at the whole Church from the pope down. It's a terrible feeling. I know. The same thing may happen on a lesser scale to those who are loyal parishioners and members of the Church. They have been generous to the point of sacrifice. They have given till it hurts - and then a new pastor or a new administrator comes, and they are completely forgotten. They know that God did not do this, but emotionally they feel that they have been rejected.

Why the Church fails

When we are thinking clearly, we see that if Church leaders fail us it is not the Mystical Body of Christ. It is not our Divine Saviour who fails us. Keep this in mind, because otherwise you will get angry at God. "I'm not going to Church anymore. God let me down." God didn't let you down. Msgr. Stoopnagle, or Sister Mary Officious, or Brother Grinch let you down. That's who let you down. They let God down, too.

The reason the Church fails us is that it is made up of human beings. The Church is a collection of people with original sin. I'm not talking about the heavenly

Church of the saints or even that part of the life of the Church where the sacraments remain untouched in their integrity because that's the way Christ instituted them. (If you receive a sacrament from a priest who is unworthy, you still receive the sacrament.) I'm not referring to the Church that gives us the Bible, the Church that certified the Old Testament and identified the books of the New Testament. I'm not referring to the apostolic teaching of the Church, given by Christ and handed on under the guidance of the Holy Spirit. It is the human side of the Church that can hurt everyone, and yet this human side also does an inestimable amount of good. At the same time, the human side can break your heart.

How can the Church of Christ fail us?

The question is obvious. How could this happen in a Church founded by Christ? The answer is to be found in the Gospels. What about the apostles? How did they do? Did they fail Jesus Christ when he needed them the most? On the very day when they were made his sacred representatives - the day he told them, "Do this in remembrance of me" - on that day they ran out on him.

The Church is made up of almost a billion people with original sin. That's a whole lot of original sin. And these billion people do extraordinarily good things -

and some of them do extraordinarily bad things. If the Catholic Church is the true Church of Christ, you should expect the greatest of saints and the worst of knaves and sinners would be in the same Church. That is what happened in the time of Christ.

What to do

We've all been hurt by people in the Church, even those in authority. When this happens, the first thing to do is to calm down. In fact, that's a good rule when you get hurt by anyone. Take a walk and calm down. The Irish have a saying, "Take counsel with your pillow", which means to sleep on it. Then ask yourself, when you calm down, "Is this really my problem? Did I expect too much from mortal human beings? Am I looking for something in the Church that legitimately I may hope for?" The answer is probably "Yes." It was reasonable, even just. But I cannot absolutely demand kind and faithful treatment, because Jesus Christ himself did not find this in the Church he established. As we have seen, the Church has always been made up of weak individuals. When we are hurt by the Church we recognise that the problem is that "the Church" can be very inconsistent. The people in the Church can be nice one day and bad the next. Even on the same day and in the same parish, there are those who can be terribly charitable and terribly unkind.

Next I ask myself the question, "Am I overly dependent on the Church? Has my reliance on Church people caused me not to rely enough on God and his Son?" You know, many people have very positive experiences in the Church. They work for the Church, and it's been a very positive experience. They went to a Catholic school, and they learned a lot. They were part of a committee or a movement or something in the Church, and it was the most positive thing they ever did in their whole lives. They think that's going to last forever. That's what you call a honeymoon, and it doesn't last. All things pass away. Don't depend on a particular part of the Church. Depend on God.

When to move

Sometimes people come to me and say, "I can't stand my parish. The sermons are not really authentic teaching of the Catholic faith." Sadly, this can happen in these times. It has happened before in Church history. And people ask me, "What do I do?" If you have a car, drive. If you don't have one, either get one or a bicycle, or a horse, or hitch a ride with a friend. Move, or buy bus tokens. Go someplace else. This is a world of transportation. If you are in a parish where you are uncomfortable because you think the people in charge are not enthusiastically loyal to the teaching of the Catholic Church presently interpreted by the

Bishop of Rome, move. People always ask me, "What should I do?" Travel.

Make your voice heard

If things aren't that bad, but are disquieting, make an intelligent noise. Unfortunately, most of the time the noises that people make are not very intelligent. I learned this because sometimes I have to follow up on complaints, and at least half the complaints are just off the deep end. They're silly or trivial or crazy. At times good complaints are submitted, but the one complaining arrives with an axe. You're trying to do the best you can to keep the local Church going, trying to represent the Mystical Body of Christ in the messy world we live in, and someone is all upset because a priest wears blue vestments in Advent or something like that. Many devout but troubled Catholics don't know how to make the distinction between someone being heretical and someone being naughty.

Christians may not be Pharisees

We must not be Pharisees. The Pharisees did not do well. They spent plenty of time and energy observing the law, but they missed the Son of God. They were there on Calvary, but they were on the wrong side.

On the other hand, we must be honest and people of integrity. It is necessary to know the difference between a dogma and a tradition. If you're going to object to something that's out of order, you need to know how important it really is. I was castigated as a young priest in the sixties when, with the written permission of the archbishop, I preached in synagogues and Protestant churches. People made fun of me, criticised me, wrote to the chancery office against me, and all the time I had the permission of Cardinal Spellman. I lived to see Pope John Paul II preach in the synagogue of Rome. I was severely criticised for doing something that within twenty years the Pope himself would do.

Being loyal even when you are hurt

Perhaps the Church has hurt you. The Church has hurt me. It has hurt most people near it for any length of time - not the whole Church, but part of it. I assure you that you and I will know, at the end of our days, that great Church which is the Mystical Body of Christ when it comes to its full reality. That is what eternal life is - when all who are saved from every nation and race and people will be gathered into the Mystical Body of Christ. We are preparing now for the heavenly Church, but our own spiritual life will be very weak and very narrow indeed if we do not loyally struggle for the Church in this world and try to be faithful to her even when others are not faithful. On Judgment Day no one is going to ask you about what anybody else did for the Church, only about what you and I did as individuals, as members of the Church of Christ in this wounded world.

Let us be faithful to that Church which our Lord Jesus Christ sent down through the ages, and let us find our spiritual fulfilment in being what St Francis, St Catherine, St Teresa, St John of the Cross, St Pius X, Padre Pio, Father Solanus, Cardinal Cooke, Pope John Paul II, and Mother Teresa all were or are in their lives - faithful, humble, generous, self-effacing members of the Church of Christ.

Chapter 5

When We Are Our Own Worst Enemies

We have considered the problems that we may have with others and our difficulties with the Church. Now we must look at the problems we have with ourselves. You may find that if you look into your own life (especially as you get older) one of the most important realizations in the process of maturation is that we bring many, if not most, of our problems on ourselves. When things don't make sense, it's often because we didn't make sense out of things. There may be some consolation in knowing that this is a general human experience. One finds the tendency to make troubles for oneself even in the lives of saints. Like the rest of us, even these special people brought on many of their own troubles. Few are exempt from being their own enemies at least some of the time. Saints, sinners, biblical personages, and even modern celebrities all gather together under the great banner that says: "Let's sink our own boat." It's one of the more obvious and universal signs of original sin that with a series of well thought out moves, carefully considered, prudently studied, and done with great expeditiousness and even prayer, we sink our boats, saints and sinners alike.

In many cases, one has to be a bit of a sinner to be one's own worst enemy. However, it is not by any means necessary. You can do this just as effectively even if you're devout - you will just do it a bit more piously. We can all say with a certain amount of conviction that "we've met the enemy and it's us".

Stepping out in faith

Just think of some of the ways a person can mess up things for himself. The most obvious is precipitous behaviour - going ahead and doing something and not considering the implications, all of the things that are going to be consequential from it. Many devout people say, "I can't figure it out, so I'm going to take the great leap of faith and jump...into an empty swimming pool." I hear people saying, "I'm going to step out in faith!" Why don't they step out in common sense at the same time? Don't blame God if you walk off the end of the dock.

The opposite mistake is thinking things out so carefully and being so cautious that we don't do what we're supposed to do. As Christians we are supposed to step out in faith, but we often sit down in confusion. Many, not knowing what to do, simply don't do anything.

Denial of reality

Another effective way to sink one's boat is to deny obvious dangers and walk into them. In psychology we speak about defence mechanisms, unconscious ways of distorting realities we think we can't cope with. Consider the successful professional who is smoking two packs a day. He has been told a thousand times, "That's very dangerous for your health." He may reply, "You know, Golda Meir used to smoke two packs a day, and she lived into her seventies." This chain smoker ignores the army of other people who smoked two packs a day and who didn't make it to fifty. We all deny obvious dangers. At this time there are appalling cracks and rifts in the Church, many signs of disunity. Yet, responsible people often deny these dangers. They pretend they're not there.

How to avoid being our own worst enemies

Failure to organise our behaviour around our everlasting goal and our God-appointed purpose in life makes us the fools that Christ speaks about in the parables. We should organise our lives around eternity to avoid self-destruction. I'm not saying that everybody should enter the cloister. That's a rare vocation. But I am saying that whatever we do, no matter what evaluation other people may make, we should consciously and purposely live every day so that it contributes to our salvation.

Another road down: going against God

Another popular road to self-destruction is indulgence in things that are forbidden. I know many who say they would like to do God's will and really consider themselves Christian, but...then comes the fine print. Of course we all sin, and sin often, out of weakness, concupiscence, feebleness, and confusion. We may even, in a stupid moment, sin with deliberate will. But knowingly and deliberately to stay on a course of action that one knows is contrary to the law of God is to open oneself for disaster. This is a commitment to sin. Many writers - from St Paul to Shakespeare to the novelist Flannery O'Connor - have said the same thing: "How blest are they that walk according to the law of the Lord and how unblest are they who do not."

Pity parties and resentment reunions

Another very effective way to defeat yourself is to keep alive all kinds of hurt feelings. If you want to live on resentment and hurt feelings, you'll have an unhealthy diet for the rest of your life, pure psychological cholesterol. How many people spend much of their energy lamenting, crying, being unhappy or sad or driving themselves literally crazy by living on resentments toward those who failed them? Yes, people do fail us. Some don't even know they're failing us; some don't mean to fail us. Some are so preoccupied with their own problems, they don't even know what they're doing. And some just don't care. The motto of the follower of Christ must be, "Keep going ahead. Don't look back." If our Lord Jesus Christ had been someone preoccupied with his own hurt feelings, none of us would have been saved. Mercifully, God does not nurse hurt feelings. For our own spiritual, as well as psychological, good, we must forgive those who trespass against us.

Waging war against oneself

We all get involved in something that has a peculiar psychological name, "passive aggression". It's very insidious. We don't know we're doing ourselves in, but we set ourselves up for disaster unconsciously. We get involved in something good or bad that's going nowhere.

Perhaps the saddest figure of all is Judas. We forget that Judas was one of the apostles. With sincerity and enthusiasm, he once chose to follow the Messiah. We may speculate that he misunderstood Christ, but so did the rest of them. Judas had the marvellous opportunity, right on the threshold of disaster, to turn back. Judas remained his own worst enemy even to the end, walking past the place of the crucifixion to hang himself. Having destroyed his reputation, the whole engagement of his life, he could have turned around and gone to Calvary and knelt at the foot of the Cross and asked for forgiveness. His conversion is the page that is not written, because Judas destroyed himself - out of self-hatred, out of resentment, out of hopelessness.

Down through the history of the Church you find many well-intentioned people who, often out of the best of motives, hurt the cause to which they have assigned their best energies. Often they are very well intentioned and actually close to God, but saints can make big mistakes, too. For example, St Francis made a terrible mistake in his life. He did it out of good will and naïveté. He let in every Tom, Dick, and Harry who came along and wanted to join his order. At the end of his life there were five thousand men in the order, and perhaps half of them should have gone home. They betrayed St Francis. They elected his worst enemy, Elias, general in his place. He let in too many men too easily. Don't think that only sinners make mistakes.

Coping with self-defeating habits

What do we do with our own self-destructive tendencies? The first and obvious thing is to admit that we may indeed be self-destructive. If you think you can't be your own worst enemy, you are easily deceived. To think that you cannot be deceived is to be already deceived, wisely observed St John of the Cross.

The first thing to do is to try to recognise those tendencies in yourself and cope with them. Trying to get rid of all self-defeating ways is probably a waste of time. But trying to curb and control these tendencies is an effective way to deal with them. Unfortunately, when we try to curb self-defeating tendencies, we inevitably run into the well-meant opposition of our friends. I'm an old-fashioned, card-carrying workaholic. I do certain things to moderate this vice. I take an hour or two off to do something interesting or educational. I may go away and give a retreat so I can get a little peace and normal sleep. Inevitably someone comes along and says, "Oh, you shouldn't do that", or else suggests or demands activity that will be burdensome.

God works with us

God is infinitely good, and he works with our self-destructiveness. He doesn't encourage it in any way, although his representatives may accidentally do so. Christ says, "Love your neighbour as yourself", which makes the assumption that you are not to hate yourself and should not be destroying yourself. However, on the other hand, if after a series of well-placed moves you find yourself going down the chute, God will be there for you. He never, ever gives up on those who let him help them. He remains there to help us even if we (wrongly) blame the problems that we have caused on him. Often we do our own will and convince ourselves that it was God's will. It was not God's will. We were like the safecracker who heard the police outside and knelt down to pray that he wouldn't get caught. We can't expect God to bail us out when we do stupid things, but we can look for him to be there when we acknowledge what we have done. He will be there. Our heavenly Father knows far better than we do that we all have neurotic and self-destructive impulses. He will be sorry for our childishness. He will remain by us. Don't ever expect to do anything perfectly, except to be perfectly stupid, but do expect that whoever calls on the name of the Lord will find him.

Receiving his merciful embrace

If we seek him sincerely and desire to please him above all things, God will accept and work with the mistakes that each one of us makes, saint or sinner. Often these require forgiveness; and his merciful

embrace is always there for us even in the worst of times. I know people who have ruined their whole lives but then found God in prison. God was there for them. And so this strange topic of self-defeat, so often experienced, so seldom discussed, ends on this note, "Do not be afraid…for the Lord your God is with you" (*Jos* 1:9). If this is not clear enough, Jesus said to his confused and self-destructive apostles, "Let not your hearts be troubled nor be afraid" (*Jn* 14:27). "Behold I am with you till the end of the world" (*Mt* 28:20). No matter what happens, believe that this is true.

Chapter 6

When Death Robs Us

We come inevitably to the most painful topic in this book, the one that causes believers to waver a bit in their firmness of faith and makes many of the weak stumble. The death of those who are dear to us, of those on whom we have relied, is life's worst pain. We must consider, at the same time, the inevitability of death - the death of those we love and our own deaths. The first thing that must be said is that it is absolutely fruitless to run away from death. There is no place to run. Every one of us, from the youngest to the eldest, is dying at exactly the same speed: twenty-four hours a day, seven days a week. We are all moving through life accompanied by the ticking of the clock. To run from death, to pretend for a time that it doesn't exist, is an utterly useless deception. Death needs to be faced and faced very squarely wherever and whoever you are.

This is not an easy thing to do, for almost everything in our culture pretends that things have to work out well and that there are no mysteries or unsolvable problems. Everything in our culture tells us to pretend that death will not come to us - although, paradoxically, the media are preoccupied by accounts of murder, war, and violent death.

At death, we all need to struggle with sorrow. This means that we have to deal with death as a reality of life before we are suddenly confronted with it.

The loss of death

Death has many dark sides to it. First of all, there is our pity for the one who is dying or has died. This is especially true if death is made difficult by reason of a protracted, painful illness or by a sudden horror like an accident or fire. We suffer along with those whom we love and are deeply frustrated that we were not able to do something for them. In our tears, grief, pain, and frustration, we say to God, "What is the use of all of this suffering? Why this innocent person? Why this child?" This is certainly part of what St Paul calls "the sting of death" (1 Co 15:56). The powerful model of this suffering is the sorrowful Mother of Christ, shown so movingly in the statue called "The Pietà", an image of pain for one who is loved.

The dark valley

Another source of grief is the mysterious dark door of death, the shadow of death, the decay of the body, the silence of the grave, the utter lack of response on the part of the dear one who has died. For the vast majority of the living, death is a dark corridor down which a dear one has passed into silence. Faith remains the only light illumining that corridor, like a searchlight beam pointed down a long tunnel, very dimly revealing the reality at the other end.

Weep for the living

Perhaps an even greater pain is the loss of the one who has been a support, or even an integral part, of one's life. Obviously, we attend the funerals of many people whom we have known and admired, but we barely saw them - and they were never an integral part of our daily struggle. At any funeral, you can easily distinguish the large group of mourners who have come to pay their respects, and even a debt of gratitude; these are those who deeply experience the loss of this particular person's influence in their lives. For the much smaller group of deeply grieved people, the pain is a pain of loss. It may be a parent grieving for a little child or a child for a parent, a husband for his wife or a very close friend who has been part of someone else's whole life. There are few people who do not experience death as a robber - one who comes with no right and deprives us of what we need, perhaps desperately. It was this deep grief that caused St Augustine to make the comment, "Weep for the living; don't weep for the dead." It is the painful loss of those we cherish that causes us to think of death as a robbery, because, with no apparent reason, it takes someone we need. We may be angry with God that he has called one whom we needed so very much. With all this in mind, let's try to make some sense of death so that we can know what to do when it comes upon us "like a thief in the night".

Getting tidied up for heaven

This is the place to say something about the much misunderstood and denied doctrine of Purgatory, what the Eastern Orthodox Christians call the place of expiation. Unfortunately, Purgatory has had a very bad press. Many people grew up with an image of Purgatory as hideous pools of fire with naked holy souls bobbing up and down like French fries in a fast-food emporium. The Council of Trent condemned making the temporal punishment in Purgatory sound hideous.

St Catherine of Genoa, who wrote a marvellous book on Purgatory, maintained on the basis of her mystical experience that it is a vast improvement over this life and that the holy souls have no regrets except that they haven't finally taken their place in heaven. For her, Purgatory is a gift of God's mercy permitting us to cooperate with his grace in removing all the obstacles that we put between ourselves and his love.

If one thinks about death, it's helpful to think about what comes after it. It stands to reason that most of us will be headed toward Purgatory, so it's not a bad idea to spend a little time thinking about that wonderful preparation for our final entrance into the Kingdom of God. If you happen to be a canonisable saint, it's not necessary to do this, but otherwise I think it is time well spent.

Death is awesome

Death confronts us with the mysterious element in life. In contemporary society, we deny the existence of the mysterious. Many things are mysterious - life, love, darkness - but what is more mysterious than eternity? If you can't cope with mystery, this life is going to drive you mad or make you cynical or terribly depressed. Life is filled with many unanswered questions. To be honest, if we did not seek answers to these questions, we'd all be sheep. Mystery gives suffering humanity its greatest dignity. Death brings us directly into an unavoidable confrontation with the mysteriousness of life. This is true whether death is expected or sudden, whether it is the welcomed death of a very ill person who longs to go home or whether it is seen as the worst possible thing - the sickness of a small child or a person who has life in front of him. When death arrives it is usually as a mystery. But what do we do in the case of this mystery? People of every religion and people in the world, every racial group, every culture - what do they do when death comes? They pray. Even unbelievers pray. They may never pray at any other time, but they pray in the presence of death, because death is what gives life some dimensions, its mystery and its meaning. Death is the frame around life. As we make our way through life we need to learn the lessons that death can teach us. For the Christian, the approach of death has a great message: Jesus Christ identified himself with us to such an extent that he was willing not only to die, but to endure a terrible and painful death.

Death is not forever

As you consider the death of those dear to you, keep in mind that death does not rob us forever. It does rob us now of someone we love and need very much. We can be very angry at death and at a God who allows it to rob us. Recall that God himself came and took up the heavy burden of a painful, miserable, horrible death by torture. While we complain, we know that he has suffered this before us. It does not answer all the questions, but the Cross does put them in perspective.

Learning from death

Death is a powerful teacher and has many lessons to teach us. Learn from death that nothing in this world lasts forever, that everything in this life passes away. Learn from death not to cling to anything in such a way that you can't go on without it. Instead, learn to refer all things to eternity. Do not be so comfortable with anything in this world that you will be unprepared to leave it. Faith gives us the immense consolation of knowing that we shall have restored to us on the other side of the grave all the good things we had in this world but in a transcendingly beautiful way. Naturally we're frightened. We don't know what death is like. "Eye has not seen, ear has not heard, it has not entered our hearts to think" (*1 Co* 2:9). But we do know, Christ tells us, "In my Father's house there are many mansions" (*Jn* 14:2).

What more loving and beneficial thing can one do for the dead than to offer the Sacrifice of Christ for them. How beautiful and consoling to pray for the dead on their journey. We have no idea what that journey is like. If they're already saints in the wonderful mystical reality of heaven, then let's pray with them. The saints live in the celebration of the

Paschal Mystery of which the Liturgy of the Mass in this world is the only substantial reflection. At the Liturgy they attend, Christ is the High Priest. Here in this world, we poor men who are called priests stand in for him according to his command.

Make up your mind to use death as we are supposed to. It can lift our eyes to eternity. And when it's a painful death, a death that may make you angry, that seems unjust and unfair - for example, an innocent person killed by malice - it is most important to pray. Then we need to remind ourselves that this innocent one has walked down a very short corridor into the light of God. However painful their dying may be, no matter how racked their bodies are with pain, the dying pass along a very short corridor. If they are prepared, they enter immediately into eternal life. We pray for loved ones on their journey that they may already be at peace with God.

Death comes to all

This chapter has been about the grief we experience when death robs us of those we love and need, but ultimately death comes to each of us. If you want, you can see it not as a robber but as a deliverance. Death comes to all. It is their shepherd, and yours and mine as well. In this we must have hope. Christ shows us that the poorest of the poor can be saved. He saves

a thief as he himself is dying on the Cross. That fact alone should give us great hope.

Death looms before us like a great door. It is awesome because it is larger than any other reality we ever face. It sums up all that has been and brings to an end all that might be yet to happen. It is a great and silent door. But for the person of faith, it becomes an inviting mystery. In the course of the years one becomes weary of conflict and sorrow. One longs for the fulfilment of the most profound needs of the human heart - for peace from conflict within and without, for a place free of danger and disappointment, for relationships untroubled by change and unmarred by selfishness. One longs to see, at last, the beauty of God, which has summoned us throughout life, shining out here and there. The words of the Psalm take on a poignant meaning as one gets older, "I have loved, O Lord, the beauty of thy house and the place where thy glory dwells" (*Ps* 26:8). One desires to embrace again loved ones gone long ago - from childhood and adolescence. Death becomes a possibility of going home to our Father's house. For the believer, it begins to lose the bitterness and sting that St Paul spoke about and begins faintly to resemble what death was supposed to be before the Fall, a passing on to a far better place, a coming home after a long journey.

Chapter 7

What Do We Do
When Everything Falls Apart?

What do we do when everything falls apart? This happens in most people's lives at least once. We all experience a month or a year or a time when nothing at all makes sense. Things we have worked hardest to accomplish, to provide for others, are destroyed overnight.

It may appear that some people are spared this experience. They seem to live lives where everything fits together, everything makes sense, everything is pleasant if not wonderful. But, as we have seen, this is an illusion because it isn't true in anyone's life. It is part of old English manners that define our customs not to share one's griefs or sorrows with others. So we all live with the illusion that everyone else is having a wonderful time. Ask others how they're doing, and they'll say, "Fine." And they'll ask you, and you will say, "Fine." None of us is doing fine at all. It's a blessing to work with the poor - they don't say, "Fine." Ask them how things are going, and they'll say, "Awful."

It often happens that those who have done the best they could in life find themselves ruined by a business collapse, by a failure in their family - perhaps a marriage that they entered into, giving their all for a lifetime, just falls apart, or someone they trusted fails them completely. People have entered into religious life only to see the community that they served fall apart. One lives surrounded by people who have been punished by life in a way that makes no sense at all. Perhaps there is that rare person (statistically this may happen) whose life goes marvellously and who finally has a nice retirement. But then he too will die. It's all going to fall apart, isn't it. Those of us who have had tough times in life say, "Oh, just another death: mine." We're prepared for it. But someone for whom life has been gentle and placid (and there are very, very few such) is going to be so shocked, so appalled that he won't quite know what to do. In the notes of Cardinal Cooke I found a little line that read, "The man who has suffered will not fear death."

A time to believe

When things fall apart and all seems to be ruined and when the terrible question "What do you do when nothing makes sense?" comes right home, the answer is that it is the time to believe. It is the time for faith. In the strongest possible New Testament sense of that word, one must believe. One must grab onto God. It's nothing abstract like: "I think there must be a God because there are such beautiful trees and stars. Where did this all come from?" No, it's nothing like that. It's powerful. It's burning. "God, you are there, and I have nothing else to cling to." One must be able to say, "I believe that God's goodness is going to bring about some greater good by this horror. It may not be a great good for me in this world, but it will be a great good someplace, somewhere, perhaps for those I love in the next world."

In your life, when things begin to fall apart, apparently by happenstance, perhaps because of the ill will of others, or on the occasion of terminal illness or death or economic insecurity or the loss of a position - when things start to fall apart, for heaven's sake, take yourself to prayer. Not prayer that is going to help you tell God what to do. That's not very helpful prayer. God already knows what to do. But prayer that will reassure you that you are in the hands of God.

The martyrs - witnesses to good out of evil

What is more distressing to us than the death of the innocent? Whether it is a Christian in ancient Rome or the Jews in Auschwitz or the bomb victims of London or Hiroshima - regardless of who caused it or why, the death of the innocent is the ultimate abomination. And people are so casual about this. Starvation, abortion, political machinations - all these cry out that something is terribly wrong. This is especially true when the victim is a child - a St Maria Goretti or an Anne Frank.

One group of victims, the martyrs, proclaim the message that all believers must hold onto in the worst situations. We often think of them as witnesses to the faith, and indeed they do give a powerful testimony to life after death. But they also remind us that God brings good out of evil. Innumerable innocent people have died because they were in the way and seemed expendable or because of the greed and sinfulness of man. The martyrs thought that the loss of life was not the ultimate disaster. We need to listen to them in order to put our experience of life into perspective. The martyrs remind us that God continues to bring immense good out of evil. We have been horrified by dreadful crimes against generous apostles in recent years - for instance, in Central America, the assassination of Archbishop Romero, the killing of the Jesuit priests, and the murder of sisters, one of whom, a Maryknoll sister, I had taught. There have been so many in this century. These were horrible, dreadful, bloodthirsty, hideous events. But out of these things, which were only permitted by God and perpetrated by the free will of human beings, he can bring immense good. As Scripture says, "Their blood cries out."

The ultimate evil leads to the ultimate good

You and I are not likely to be martyred. We have not earned such a glorious fate. But we'll probably die of the things people ordinarily die of - strokes, heart attacks, cancer, getting hit by a car or even - in this crazy world - by a stray bullet. But we will die, and the majority of us will know that we're dying when we're dying. This will give us the same opportunity that the martyr has to surrender ourselves freely to God. The ultimate natural evil of this life is death - it ends our biological existence. It is also the opportunity for the ultimate victory, which is eternal life. St Paul put it so well, "Death, where is your victory? Death where is your sting?" (1 Co 15:55). The ultimate evil leads to the ultimate good. Yes, the door to eternity is a low, dark door called death. The corridor to the other side is apparently very short, so short indeed that the very saintly often describe their oncoming death with these words, "The Lord will come for me."

My Redeemer - your Redeemer - has the right to be called that because he suffered with us as well as for us. God could have saved us in some simpler, less terrible way than subjecting himself to the worst that human beings could do, but he wanted us to know how much he loved us when we are in pain and suffering. Salvation surely did not need to come through the murder of the Messiah. But that's how it came, so we could know, in all sufferings and sorrows of life, that our Creator was also our Redeemer, that he would bring joy out of sorrow, hope out of despair, love out of hate, life out of death, eternity out of time. This is our hope. It alone makes sense.

Chapter 8

Prayers And Thoughts
For Dark Times

When one is struggling to go on in dark times and trials, it is often most helpful to cling to a prayer or thought. The following prayers and thoughts, arranged around the needs we have discussed, may be helpful.

God is with me
For God alone (Psalm 62:5-7)

For God alone my soul waits in silence; from him comes my salvation.

He only is my rock and my salvation, my fortress; I shall not be greatly moved.

On God rests my deliverance and my honour; my mighty rock, my refuge is God.

Trust in him at all times, O people; pour out your heart before him; God is refuge for us.

Do not worry
(*Matthew* 6:25-33)

Therefore I tell you, do not be anxious about your life, what you shall eat or what you shall drink, nor about your body, what you shall put on. Is not life more than food and the body more than clothing? Look at the birds of the air: they neither sow nor reap nor gather into barns, and yet your heavenly Father feeds them. Are you not of more value than they? And which of you by being anxious can add one cubit to his span of life? And why are you anxious about clothing? Consider the lilies of the field, how they grow; they neither toil nor spin; yet I tell you, even Solomon in all his glory was not arrayed like one of these. But if God so clothes the grass of the field, which today is alive and tomorrow is thrown into the oven, will he not much more clothe you, O men of little faith? Therefore do not be anxious, saying, 'What shall we eat?' or 'What shall we drink?' or 'What shall we wear?' For the Gentiles seek all these things; and your heavenly Father knows that you need them all. But seek first his kingdom and his righteousness, and all these things shall be yours as well.

When all seems dark
Most high, glorious God

Most high, glorious God, lighten the darkness of my
heart and grant me, Lord,
a correct faith, a certain hope,
a perfect charity,
and sense of knowledge, so that I may carry out
Your holy and true command.

(*St Francis of Assisi*)

And Job Said
(*Job* 3:2-6, 20-26)

And Job said, "Let the day perish wherein I was born,
and the night which said, 'A man-child is conceived.'
Let that day be darkness! May God above not seek it,
nor light shine upon it. Let gloom and deep darkness
claim it. Let clouds dwell upon it; let the blackness of
the day terrify it. That night - let thick darkness seize it!
let it not rejoice among the days of the year, let it not
come into the number of the months.

"Why is light given to him that is in misery, and
life to the bitter in soul, who long for death and it
comes not, and dig for it more than for hid treasures;
who rejoice exceedingly, and are glad, when they find
the grave? Why is light given to a man whose way is
hid, whom God has hedged in? For my sighing comes
as my bread, and my groanings are poured out like

water. For the thing that I fear comes upon me, and what I dread befalls me. I am not at ease, nor am I quiet; I have no rest; but trouble comes."

Trusting in God
I cannot be thrown away

1. God was all-complete, all-blessed in himself; but it was his will to create a world for his glory. he is Almighty, and might have done all things himself, but it has been his will to bring about his purposes by the beings he has created. We are all created to his glory - we are created to do his will. I am created to do something or to be something for which no one else is created; I have a place in God's counsels, in God's world, which no one else has; whether I be rich or poor, despised or esteemed by man, God knows me and calls me by my name.

2. God has created me to do him some definite service; he has committed some work to me which he has not committed to another. I have my mission - I never may know it in this life, but I shall be told it in the next. Somehow I am necessary for his purposes, as necessary in my place as an archangel in his - if, indeed, I fail, he can raise another, as he could make the stones children of Abraham. Yet I have a part in this great work; I am a link in a chain,

a bond of connexion between persons. He has not created me for naught. I shall do good, I shall do his work; I shall be an angel of peace, a preacher of truth in my own place, while not intending it, if I do but keep his commandments and serve him in my calling.

3. Therefore I will trust him. Whatever, wherever I am, I can never be thrown away. If I am in sickness, my sickness may serve him; in perplexity, my perplexity may serve him; if I am in sorrow, my sorrow may serve him. My sickness, or perplexity, or sorrow may be necessary causes of some great end, which is quite beyond us. He does nothing in vain; he may prolong my life, he may shorten it; he knows what he is about. He may take away my friends, he may throw me among strangers, he may make me feel desolate, make my spirits sink, hide the future from me - still he knows what he is about.

O Adonai, O Ruler of Israel, thou that guidedst Joseph like a flock, O Emmanuel, O Sapientia, I give myself to thee. I trust thee wholly. Thou art wiser than I - more loving to me than I myself. Deign to fulfil thy high purposes in me whatever they be - work in and through me. I am born to serve thee, to be thine, to be thy instrument. Let me be thy blind instrument. I ask not to see - I ask not to know - I ask simply to be used.

(*Bl. John Henry Cardinal Newman*)

Prayers in time of sickness
Prayers of a shepherd of souls
(Attributed to Terence Cardinal Cooke)

For a sick person

Almighty God, giver of health and healing, grant to Your servant a palpable sense of your presence and perfect trust in you. In suffering may he cast his care on you, so that, enfolded in your love and power, he may receive health and salvation according to your gracious will. Through Christ our Lord. Amen.

For one's self when ill

Dear Lord, you are the greatest physician. I turn to you in my sickness and ask you to help me. Put your hand upon me as you did for the people long ago and let health and wholeness come into me from you. I put myself under your care and affirm my faith that even now your marvellous healing grace is making me well and strong again.

I know that I ask more than I deserve, but you never measure our benefits on that basis. You just love us back into health. Do that for me. I earnestly ask and I will try to serve you more faithfully. This I promise through Christ our Lord. Amen.

Prayer when worried

Dear Lord, I'm worried and full of fear. Anxiety and apprehension fill my mind. Could it be that my love for you is weak and imperfect and as a result I am plagued by worry?

I have tried to reassure myself that there is nothing to worry about. But such reassurances do not seem to help. I know that I should just rest myself confidently on your loving care and guidance. But I have been too upset even to pray. Touch me, dear Lord, with your peace, and help my disturbed spirit to know that you are God and that I need fear no evil.

Before an operation

Loving Father, I entrust myself to your care this day; guide with wisdom and skill the minds and hands of those who heal in your name. Grant that with every cause of illness removed, I may be restored to sound health and learn to live in more perfect harmony with you and with my neighbour. Through Jesus Christ. Amen.

For the depressed person

Praise to you, O Christ, and honour and glory! As your Passion drew nearer, you began to know weariness and depression. Thus you took upon yourself the weakness of our human nature that you might strengthen and console those who are fearful of serious illness. I beg you to free me from all discouragement and anxiety. Grant that all I endure may be to your glory and for the pardon of my sins. Deliver me from faintheartedness and all unreasonable fears, and fix my heart firmly and unwaveringly on you. Amen.

The changeless friend

The friendship of Jesus

Alone I was, without a single friend to give me a word of encouragement, I could neither pray nor read, but there I remained, for hours and hours together, uneasy in mind and afflicted in spirit, on account of the weight of my trouble, and of the fear that perhaps after all I was being tricked by the devil, and wondering what in the world I could do for my relief. Not a gleam of hope seemed to shine upon me from either earth or heaven; except just this that in the midst of all my fears and dangers I never forgot how Our Lord must be seeing the weight of all I endured.

O my Lord Jesus Christ! What a true friend you are, and how powerful! For when you wish to be with us you can be, and you always do wish it if only we will receive you. May everything created, O Lord of all the world, praise you and bless you! If only I could tramp the whole world over, proclaiming everywhere with all the strength that is in me what a faithful friend you are to those who will be friends with you! My dear Lord, all else fails and passes away; you, the Lord of them all, never fail, never pass away. What you allow those who love you to suffer is all too little. O my Lord, how kindly, how nobly, how tenderly, how sweetly, you succeed in handling and making sure of your own! Oh, if only one could secure that one would love nothing but just you alone! You seem, my dear Lord, to put to the trial with rods and agonies one who loves you, only that, just when you have brought her to the last extreme of endurance, she may understand all the more the boundless limits of your love.

(*St Thérèse of Lisieux*)

The mercy of God
Psalm 57:1–3

Be merciful to me, O God, be merciful to me, for in thee my soul takes refuge; in the shadow of thy wings I will take refuge, till the storms of destruction pass by.

I cry to God Most High, to God who fulfils his
purpose for me.

He will send from heaven and save me, he will put
to shame those who trample upon me. God will send
forth his steadfast love and his faithfulness.

Wisdom 15:1–3

But thou, our God, art kind and true, patient and
ruling all things in mercy.

For even if we sin we are thine, knowing thy power;
but we will not sin, because we know that we are
accounted thine.

For to know thee is complete righteousness, and to
know thy power is the root of immortality.

We know not what is good for us

Ah, Lord, we know not what is good for us, and what
is bad. We cannot foretell the future, nor do we know
when thou comest to visit us, in what form thou wilt
come. And therefore, we leave it all to thee. Do thou
thy good pleasure to us and in us. Let us ever look at
thee, and do thou look upon us, and give us the grace
of thy bitter cross and Passion, and console us in thy
own way and at thy own time.

(Bl. John Henry Cardinal Newman)

At the death of a loved one
They do not forget us

Not long after our conversion and regeneration by your baptism, you took him from this life, by then a baptised Catholic and serving you in Africa in perfect chastity among his own people, for he had made his whole family Christian. And now he lives in Abraham's bosom. Whatever is meant by that bosom, there my Nebridius lives, my most beloved friend, Your son by adoption and no longer a freed-man only. There he lives. For what other place is there for such a soul? There he lives, in the place of which he asked me, an ignorant poor creature, so many questions. He no longer puts his bodily ear to my lips, but the lips of his spirit to your fountain, drinking his fill of wisdom, all that his thirst requires, happy without end. Nor do I think he is so intoxicated with the draught of that wisdom as to forget me, since you, O Lord of whom he drinks, are mindful of all.

(St Augustine)

Prayer for the departing soul

O Lord Jesus Christ, you said through the mouth of the prophet, "I have loved you with an everlasting love: therefore in pity have I drawn you to myself." Deign, I implore you, to offer up and show to God, the Father almighty, on behalf of your servant, N., that love of yours which drew you down from heaven to earth to endure all your bitter sufferings. Deliver him (her) from all the pains and sufferings which he (she) fears that he (she) deserves for his (her) sins. and grant salvation to his (her) soul in this hour when it takes its departure. Open to him (her) the gates of life, and cause him (her) to rejoice with Your saints in everlasting glory. And do you, most loving Lord Jesus Christ, who redeemed us by your most precious blood, take pity on the soul of this your servant, N., and lead him (her) into the lovely places of paradise that are forever green so that he (she) may live with you in undivided love, never to be separated from you and from those whom you chose. You who with the Father and the Holy Spirit live and reign, God, for ever and ever. Amen.

(The Roman Ritual)

Prayer for one who has taken his own life

Crucified Saviour, there is no place for me to go but to the foot of your cross. I feel desolation, defeat, betrayal, rejection. I tried. I tried to stop the flood, to calm the earthquake, to put out the raging fire. I did not even know how desperate it all was. There is absolutely no consolation, no answer, no softening of my grief. It is complete darkness. I grieve for my dear friend [or relative], for what was and what could have been. Is life so awful that all struggle had to end, that defeat was inevitable? There is nothing but silence outside and screaming inside. I know that the wound will heal, but now I don't even want it to. I know that there will be a huge scar in its place. That scar will be all that I have left.

I am filled with terror for the one I loved and cared for. Salvation. If only I was certain of salvation for the one who is gone, defeated by this life. There is no one I can come to but you - Crucified One. Your prayer of dereliction, which always puzzled me before, now is the only thing with any meaning at all. I put my dear one whose body is destroyed into your hands. Reach down from the cross and embrace this wounded and broken soul. You descended into hell. Find our friend on the edge and rescue the one who has gone from us. We have no place to go in the world, in the whole universe but here to you, to your cross - it is our only hope. Into your hands, O Lord, we commend this spirit. Amen.

In Paradisium

May the angels lead you into paradise; may the martyrs come to welcome you on your way, and lead you into the holy city, Jerusalem. May the choir of angels welcome you and with Lazarus who once was poor may you have everlasting rest.

(*The Roman Ritual*)

Has this book helped you?
Spread the word!

@CTSpublishers

/CTSpublishers

ctscatholiccompass.org

Let us know!
marketing@ctsbooks.org
+44 (0)207 640 0042

Learn, love, live your faith.
www.CTSbooks.org